only some big cats can roar

© Aladdin Books Ltd 1999
Produced by
Aladdin Books Ltd
28 Percy Street
London W1P 0LD

First published in the United States in 1999 by
Copper Beech Books,
an imprint of
The Millbrook Press
2 Old New Milford Road
Brookfield, Connecticut 06804

Concept, editorial, and design by
David West Children's Books

Designer: Flick Killerby

Illustrators: Peter Barrett – Artist Partners,
Jonathan Pointer – Illustration Ltd., Jo Moore

Printed in Belgium
5 4 3 2 1

Cataloging-in-Publication data is on file at the
Library of Congress.

ISBN 0-7613-0900-4 (lib.bdg.)
ISBN 0-7613-0787-7 (trade hardcover)

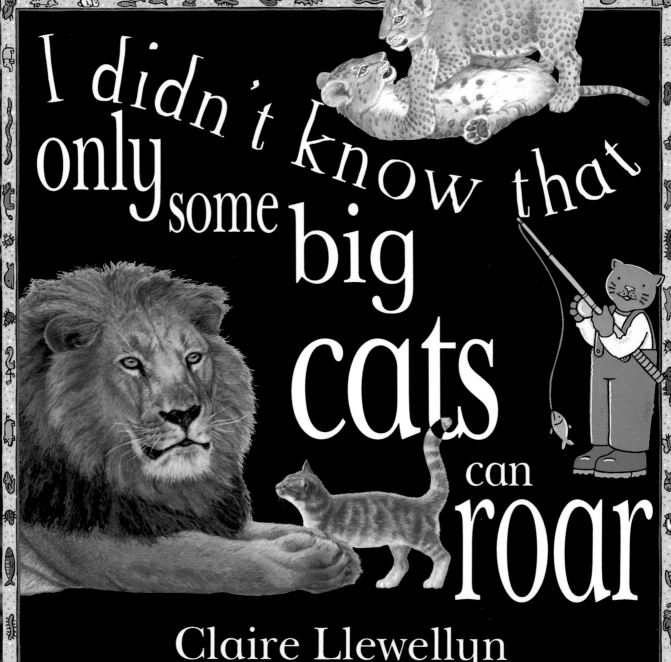

I didn't know that
only some big cats can roar

Claire Llewellyn

COPPER BEECH BOOKS
BROOKFIELD, CONNECTICUT

I didn't know that

Introduction

Did *you* know that small cats can't roar? ... that a large pride can contain up to 35 lions? ... that tigers are good swimmers?

Discover for yourself amazing facts about big cats – from snow leopards in the Himalayas to jaguars in South America and more.

Watch for this symbol that means there is a fun project for you to try.

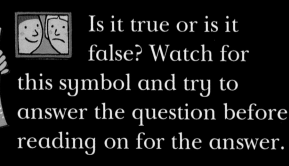

Is it true or is it false? Watch for this symbol and try to answer the question before reading on for the answer.

Don't forget to check the borders for extra amazing facts.

I didn't know that

lions are related to pet cats.

Lions and pet cats are both beautiful animals with fine fur, pointed ears, and long whiskers. Lions and cats belong to the same animal family, the *Felidae*, and behave in many similar ways.

There are 35 kinds of cats. They fit into four groups: great cats, small cats, clouded leopards, and cheetahs (above). The cheetah has its own group because it runs faster and can't pull in its claws.

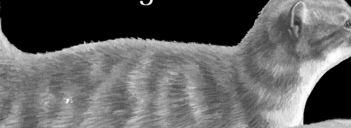

The *domestic cat* is the only cat to mix happily with humans.

A saber-toothed tiger stabbed its prey with its long teeth, then waited for it to die. They lived over 5 million years ago but died out at the end of the *Ice Age*.

I didn't know that

big cats are the top *predators.* The big cats hunt many kinds of animals, such as wild pigs, zebra, and deer, but are not hunted themselves. This makes them the top predator in the *food chain.*

A cat's long tongue is covered by small, horny spikes called papillae. These help the animal to scrape off the last bits of meat and lick the bones clean.

Tigers enjoy eating crabs, frogs, and fish.

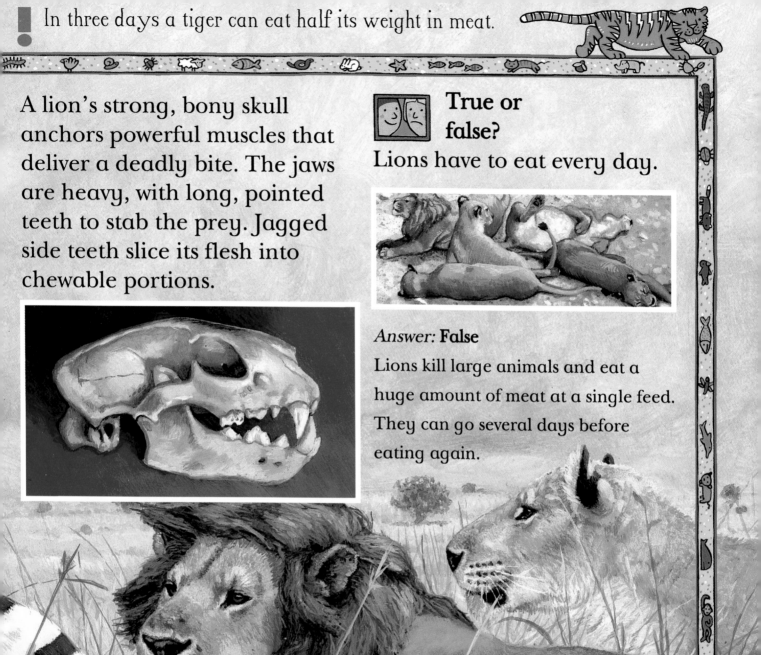

A lion's strong, bony skull anchors powerful muscles that deliver a deadly bite. The jaws are heavy, with long, pointed teeth to stab the prey. Jagged side teeth slice its flesh into chewable portions.

True or false?

Lions have to eat every day.

Answer: **False**

Lions kill large animals and eat a huge amount of meat at a single feed. They can go several days before eating again.

A leopard often drags its kill up into a tree, where it will be safe from wild dogs, hyenas, and other hungry animals. The food lasts the leopard several days.

I didn't know that

a tiger hunts on its own.

A tiger stalks its prey silently, creeping closer and closer before going for the kill. All cats' eyes face forward on the front of the head. This helps them to judge distances accurately.

10

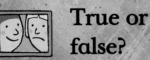 **True or false?**

Cats' eyes light up the road.

Answer: **True**

The glass road markers that reflect car headlights are known as cats' eyes.

Cats can see in the dark. Their large eyes collect as much of the dim light as possible, and then boost it with the *tapetum*, a special shiny layer at the back of the eye.

Cats have sharp, hooked claws that pin down and cut their prey. The claws can be pulled up inside the paws, so that cats can move silently on super-soft pads.

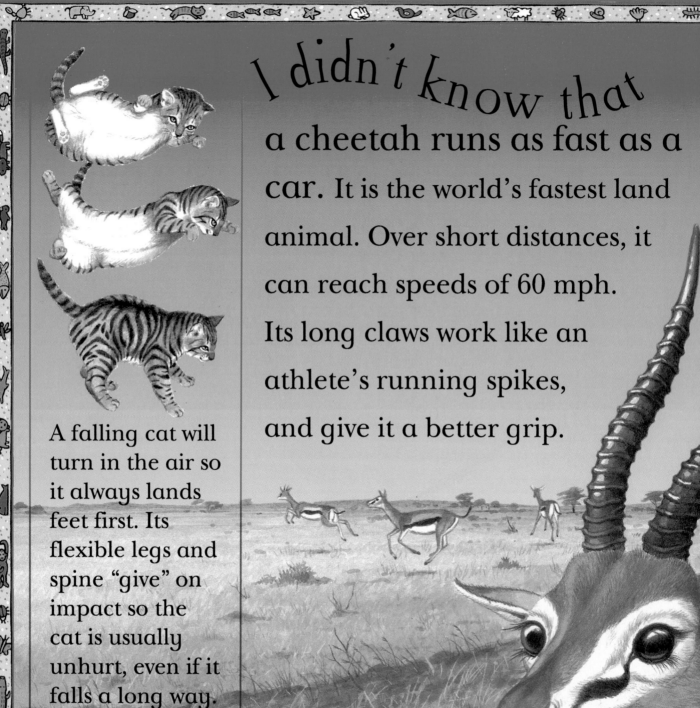

I didn't know that

a cheetah runs as fast as a car. It is the world's fastest land animal. Over short distances, it can reach speeds of 60 mph. Its long claws work like an athlete's running spikes, and give it a better grip.

A falling cat will turn in the air so it always lands feet first. Its flexible legs and spine "give" on impact so the cat is usually unhurt, even if it falls a long way.

12

The cheetah has a strong but supple spine. As the backbone flexes, the cat stretches its long, slim legs into an incredible, elongated stride.

True or false?
Cats can't swim.

Answer: **False**
Tigers are good swimmers. They often go into rivers and streams to cool off or chase their prey.

SEARCH & FIND
Can you find the capybara?
FIND & SEARCH

True or false?
Panthers don't have spots.

Answer: **False**

Panthers have a black coat, but in bright light you can still see their spots.

I didn't know that

some cats wear jungle *camouflage*. Jaguars live in the hot, steamy rainforests of South America. Their spotted coat makes perfect camouflage. It blends in with the forest's dappled light and hides them as they hunt.

The tiger (above) lives in grasslands and forests. Its stripes help to hide it in the tall grass, and the changing forest light.

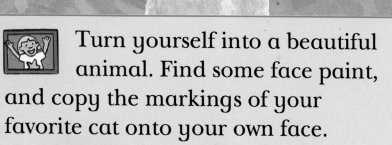

Turn yourself into a beautiful animal. Find some face paint, and copy the markings of your favorite cat onto your own face.

I didn't know that

lion cubs have spots. Lion cubs are born with a woolly coat covered in dark spots. The markings make good camouflage, and hide the cubs in the underbrush when their mother goes to hunt. The lioness hunts for food for herself; young cubs feed only on milk.

True or false?

A lioness carries her cubs in her mouth.

Answer: **True**
A lioness gently bites the loose skin around her cub's neck and carries it in her mouth.

A lioness usually has two to four cubs.

Lion cubs spend a lot of their time playing. They wrestle and chase one another or stalk their mother's twitching tail. This is a good way to train for hunting.

Cheetah cubs (above) start to eat meat when they are about six weeks old. At this time their mother needs to kill twice as much prey as she would usually need just for herself.

True or false?
Richard I of England was called the Lionhearted.

Answer: **True**
Richard I (1157-1199) was nicknamed the Lionhearted because he was a brave soldier.

Half brother

Daughter of lioness

Cousin

Half sister

Young male

SEARCH & FIND
Can you find the five lion cubs?
FIND & SEARCH

I didn't know that lions are the only cats to live in groups. Most cats live alone. Lions live in "prides." Each has one or two males, five or six females, and a number of cubs.

A large pride contains up to 35 lions of varying ages.

A pride of lions lives and hunts in its own *territory*. The males defend the territory by marking its borders with *urine* or dung and attacking strange lions that dare to appear.

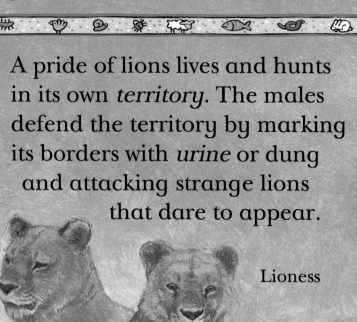

Lioness

Mother of lioness

Dominant male

Female lion cubs stay in the same pride all their lives. So the females in a pride are usually related to each other. Sisters, aunts, nieces, and cousins all help with each other's cubs, and will even give them milk.

I didn't know that

only some big cats can roar. Small cats can purr, but they can't roar. Lions, tigers, leopards, and jaguars can all roar. Cheetahs can't. Big cats often roar at dawn and dusk to warn other cats to stay away from their territory.

A lion's roar is very loud – you can hear it up to five miles away.

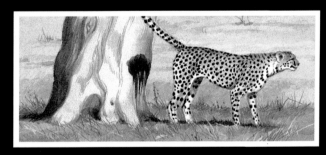

Like many cats, a cheetah marks its territory with scent. It backs up to trees and sprays them with urine. It's the cat's way of telling strangers to "Keep Out."

Try to make a pet cat purr. All you have to do is stroke it. Cats purr when they are contented, and females purr as their kittens feed.

True or false?
Lions use their tails as flags.

Answer: **True**

When it is hunting in long grass, a lion holds up its tufted tail for other lions to follow.

True or false?

Tigers live only in *tropical* lands.

Answer: **False**

The Siberian tiger lives in icy Siberia in eastern Russia. The animal is larger than tropical tigers and has a thick, shaggy coat of fur.

The puma (left) lives in the mountains of North America, where winters are often severe. The cat's large, thick paws help it to balance on icy slopes as it bounds after snowshoe hares. It also hunts elk and sheep.

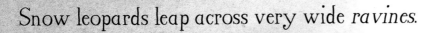

Snow leopards leap across very wide *ravines*.

Lynx (right) spend the winter in pine forests, sheltering from the worst of the weather. Although they are one of the smaller cats, they have very big, furry feet.

Cats wear two coats: a layer of soft wool close to their skin for warmth and a top layer of coarse hair that keeps out moisture.

I didn't know that

some cats wear snowshoes.

The rare snow leopard lives high in the Himalayan mountains. During the winter it grows thick fur on its feet to broaden them, and prevent them from sinking in the snow.

The *ancestor* of pet cats is the African wildcat.

SEARCH & FIND
FIND
Can you find five fish?

The caracal lives in dry places in Africa and Southwest Asia. It is a clever bird catcher, leaping high into the air to bat birds with its paws.

The North American bobcat (right) spends its day in a den and hunts at night. It is one of the smaller cats and has a short tail.

True or false?
People once worshiped cats as gods.

Answer:
True
In ancient Egypt, the goddess Bastet was represented in drawings as a cat. Because of this, all cats were sacred.

I didn't know that some cats can fish. The fishing cat of India and Southeast Asia uses its paws to scoop fish out of the water. It will even dive into the water to catch them in its mouth.

Small cats can't roar.

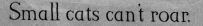

Lions were once trained to perform in circuses. People enjoyed seeing powerful animals tamed. Today, this is becoming less common.

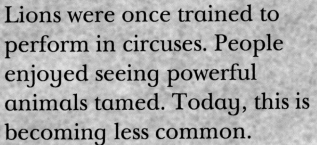

In Roman times, Christians and criminals were made to fight lions in public arenas. They must have been gory shows.

26

I didn't know that

lions sometimes attack people. Lions that are old, injured, or sick are too slow to catch their prey. Eventually, hunger and illness may drive the animals to approach villages and attack people. The problem is serious but quite rare.

SEARCH & FIND
Can you find the man with the gun?
FIND & SEARCH

Hungry tigers usually attack from behind. In the hope of preventing attacks, Indian forest workers wear face masks on the back of their head.

During the late 1800s tiger-hunting was a sport. Today, it is against the law, but poachers still kill tigers and sell their bones to make traditional *Chinese medicines*.

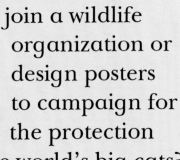

Endangered animals can't speak but you can. Why not join a wildlife organization or design posters to campaign for the protection of the world's big cats?

I didn't know that

some tigers wear collars.

In national parks in Nepal, tigers have been fitted with special collars that give out radio signals. By tracking the signals, scientists can follow the tigers and learn about the way they behave.

Many cats are facing extinction because they are killed for their fur. The skins are made into rugs and coats, and are then sold all over the world.

Glossary

Ancestor
A member of the same family that lived and died a long time ago.

Camouflage
The colors and markings on a cat's fur, which help it to blend in with its surroundings.

Chinese medicine
Traditional medicines from China, which are made from plants and animal body parts.

Domestic cat
A pet cat.

Felidae
The animal group to which all cats belong.

Food chain
A food chain shows the feeding links between living things. Each "link" in a food chain is eaten by the next. For example, grass is eaten by zebras, which are eaten by lions.

Hyena
A doglike animal from Africa and Asia that feeds on dead meat.

Ice Age

A period between two million and 10,000 years ago, when ice sheets sometimes covered large parts of the earth.

Leo (Latin for lion)

A star pattern in the sky that roughly makes the shape of a lion.

Predator

An animal that kills and eats other animals.

Ravine

A deep, narrow gorge with very steep sides.

Tapetum

The shiny part at the back of a cat's eye that helps it to see in the dark.

Territory

An area of land that a cat treats as its own and defends against other cats.

Tropical

Tropical lands are the warmest parts of the world, to the north and south of the Equator.

Urine

A strong-smelling, liquid waste from the body.

Index